WRITING STYLES
TABLE OF CON

MW01155049

WRITING STYLES: GRADE 2
INTRODUCTION

The Writing Process includes five stages:

Prewriting
Students think about topics, choose an idea, decide what kind of writing to do, make notes about the topic, and put the ideas in order.

Drafting
Students write quickly during this stage. They do not worry about mistakes.

Responding and Revising
Students read the writing to themselves or to partners. This is the stage to improve the writing.

Proofreading
Students read the writing again. They check to see that capitalization and punctuation are used correctly.

Publishing
Students share their writing with others.

This book is designed to give students practice in all stages of the writing process to help them become better writers.

ORGANIZATION OF UNIT
Each unit is organized to provide maximum practice in the writing process. Each unit begins with an assessment. Then, two lessons are provided for activities in the thinking, or *prewriting*, stage. Activities include using details to tell the main idea, grouping ideas by topic, picturing events, paying attention to details, thinking about what might happen, and connecting ideas in sequence.

The third lesson provides practice in the writer's craft. Activities include using exact words, using synonyms, writing for your reader, using colorful words, using enough details, and getting the reader's interest. Some units include a lesson that provides practice in revising. Activities include joining sentences and adding describing words to sentences.

The next type of lesson gives students practice proofreading.

Finally, each unit ends with eight to twelve writing prompts for students to practice writing. Many of these are cooperative activities for students to do in pairs or in small groups.

ORGANIZATION OF BOOK
The book is organized into six units that focus on essential types of writing: sentence about a picture, personal story, friendly letter, paragraph that describes, story, and how-to paragraph.

SENTENCE ABOUT A PICTURE
- tells a complete thought.
- begins with a capital letter.
- ends with a special mark.

A PERSONAL STORY
- tells about something you have done.
- can tell how you feel about something.
- tells what happened in order.

A FRIENDLY LETTER
- has five parts: heading, greeting, body, closing, and signature.

A PARAGRAPH THAT DESCRIBES

- tells what someone or something is like.
- has a topic sentence that names the topic.
- has other sentences that give details about the topic.

A STORY

- has a beginning, a middle, and an ending.
- is often about solving a problem.
- has a title.

A HOW-TO PARAGRAPH

- tells how to do or make something.
- has a topic sentence that names the topic of the paragraph.
- has detail sentences that explain the steps in order.
- is indented.

USE

The activities in this book are designed for independent use by students who have had instruction in the specific skills covered in the lessons. Copies of the activity sheets can be given to individuals or pairs of students for completion. When students are familiar with the content of the worksheets, they can be assigned as homework.

To begin, determine the implementation that fits your students' needs and your classroom structure. The following plan suggests a format for this implementation.

1. **Administer** *the Assessment Test to establish baseline information on each student. This test may also be used as a post-test when the student has completed a unit.*

2. **Explain** *the purpose of the worksheets to the class.*

3. **Review** *the mechanics of how you want students to work with the activities. Do you want them to work in pairs? Are the activities for homework?*

4. **Introduce** *students to the process and purpose of the activities. Work with students when they have difficulty. Give them only a few pages at a time to avoid pressure.*

ADDITIONAL NOTES

1. **Parent Communication.** *Send the Letter to Parents home with students.*

2. **Bulletin Board.** *Display completed worksheets to show student progress.*

3. **Skills Correlation and Curriculum Correlation.** *These charts indicate specific skills incorporated in the activities to help you in your daily lesson planning.*

4. **Student Progress Charts.** *Duplicate the grid charts found on pages 7-8. Record student names in the left column. Note date of completion of each lesson for each student.*

Dear Parent:

    During this school year, our class will be working on writing skills. We will be completing activity sheets that provide practice in the writing skills that can help your child become a better writer. The types of writing we will be focusing on are: a sentence about a picture, personal story, friendly letter, paragraph that describes, story, and how-to paragraph.

    From time to time, I may send home activity sheets. To best help your child, please consider the following suggestions:
- Provide a quiet place to work.
- Go over the directions together.
- Encourage your child to do his or her best.
- Check the lesson when it is complete.
- Go over your child's work, and note improvements as well as problems.

    Help your child maintain a positive attitude about writing. Provide as many opportunities for your child to write as possible. Encourage your child to keep a writer's journal. A journal is like a diary. In it, your child can draw pictures of and write about things that happen each day. Encourage your child to keep a running list of writing ideas. This can be a list of topics or story ideas for future writing projects. Display your child's writing and read the stories as a part of bedtime story time. Above all, enjoy this time you spend with your child. He or she will feel your support, and skills will improve with each activity completed.

    Thank you for your help!
    Cordially,

SKILLS CORRELATION

	Assessment	Thinking	Writer's Craft	Revising	Proofreading	Practice
Sentence About a Picture	9	10, 11	12		13	14, 15, 16, 17, 18, 19, 20, 21
Personal Story	22	23, 24	25		26	27, 28, 29, 30, 31, 32, 33, 34
Friendly Letter	35	36, 37	38	39	40	41, 42, 43, 44, 45, 46, 47, 48
Paragraph That Describes	49	50, 51	52	53	54	55, 56, 57, 58, 59, 60, 61, 62, 63, 64, 65, 66
Story	67	68, 69	70		71	72, 73, 74, 75, 76, 77, 78, 79, 80
How-to Paragraph	81	82, 83	84	85	86	87, 88, 89, 90, 91, 92, 93, 94

CURRICULUM CORRELATION

	Social Studies	Science	Literature/ Language Arts	Art/ Dramatics	Physical Education	Nutrition
Sentence About a Picture	11, 16, 17, 18, 21	12, 13, 20	10	19	15	9, 11, 14
Personal Story	22, 23, 28, 29, 30, 34	22, 24, 26, 27	32		31	25, 33
Friendly Letter	39, 43, 44, 46, 48	35, 38, 41, 45		37, 39, 40, 47	36, 42	
Paragraph That Describes	52, 56, 61, 64, 65, 66	50, 51, 55, 59, 62, 64	57	49, 53, 54, 57, 60	58	51, 63
Story	69, 75	70, 73, 74, 77, 78, 80	67, 68, 71, 72, 76, 79, 80			
How-to Paragraph	81, 86, 88, 90, 91, 93	84, 89		82, 92, 94	85, 87	83

STUDENT PROGRESS CHART

Student Name	Unit 1 Sentence About a Picture												Unit 2 Personal Story												Unit 3 Friendly Letter												
	1	2	3	4	5	6	7	8	9	10	11	12	1	2	3	4	5	6	7	8	9	10	11	12	1	2	3	4	5	6	7	8	9	10	11	12	13

STUDENT PROGRESS CHART

Student Name	Unit 4 Paragraph That Describes																	Unit 5 Story													Unit 6 How-To Paragraph												
	1	2	3	4	5	6	7	8	9	10	11	12	13	14	15	16	17	1	2	3	4	5	6	7	8	9	10	11	12	13	1	2	3	4	5	6	7	8	9	10	11	12	13

Writing Styles 2, SV 8055-3

Name _____   Date _____

UNIT 1: Sentence About a Picture
Assessment

Look at each picture. Draw a line around the group of words that is a complete sentence.

1.

The girl eats pizza.

a slice of pizza

2.

a robot and a dog

The robot walks a dog.

Finish the sentence with the more exact word.

3.

_____

- -

Mai eats _____ for breakfast.

(cereal, food)

Studying a Sentence About a Picture

- A sentence tells a complete thought.
- It begins with a capital letter.
- It ends with a special mark.

Look at each picture. Draw a line around the group of words that is a complete sentence.

1.

The balloon goes up.

man in it

2.

a messy room

The room is a mess!

3.

It's a windy fall day.

an open store

4.

a good lunch

The girl is ready to eat.

Name _____ Date _____

Using Details to Tell the Main Idea

- To write a sentence about a picture, good writers look at all the details first.
- Then they put the details together to tell the main idea.

Look at the pictures. Draw a line under the details you see in the pictures. Then draw a line under the sentence that tells the main idea.

1.

Details

fruit bowl	2 eggs
bird cage	1 glass
bedroom	2 sinks

Main Idea

One person will eat breakfast.
Fruit tastes really good!

2.

Details

ticket booth	Ferris wheel
monkeys	children
roller coaster	cotton candy

Main Idea

The fair is open!
I lost my ticket!

Name _____ Date _____

Using Exact Words

• Good writers use exact words to give a reader more information.

Finish each sentence with the more exact word.

(Animals, Chimpanzees)

_____

- -

1. _____ sit in the trees.

(looking, hunting)

_____

- -

2. They are _____ for food.

(Bananas, Fruits)

_____

- -

3. _____ are the best.

(bright, yellow)

_____

- -

4. Can they see those big _____ bunches?

(leap, move)

_____

- -

5. Watch the chimpanzees _____ !

Name _____ Date _____

Proofreading Sentences

PROOFREADING HINT
- Be sure your sentence begins with a capital letter.
- Be sure your sentence ends with a special mark.

Read each sentence. Use the Proofreader's Marks to correct the six mistakes. Write the sentences correctly.

Proofreader's Marks
≡ Use a capital letter.
⊙ Add a period.
∧ Add something.
⟋ Take out something.
⌃ Change something.
◯ Check the spelling.

1. bears are big animals.

2. They may weigh 1,000 pounds

3. some live in cold places

4. others like warm weather.

1. _____

2. _____

3. _____

4. _____

My Favorite Food

Draw a picture of your favorite food. Think of a sentence about it. Write the sentence. Show your picture to the class. Read your sentence aloud. Tell what makes it a complete sentence.

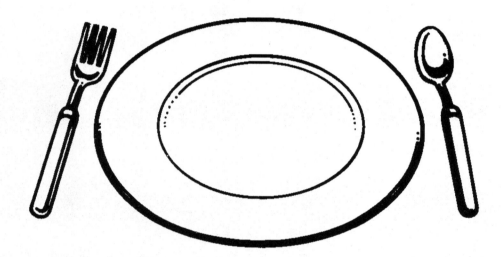

Name _____   Date _____

First Place

Imagine that you just won first place in your favorite sport. What prize did you win? Draw a picture of your prize. Write a sentence to tell about your picture.

_____

_____

_____

_____

Unit 1: Sentence About a Picture
Writing Styles 2, SV 8055-3

Going on an Outing

Think of some place you would like to go with your class. Draw a picture of the place. Then write a sentence about it.

_____

_ _

_____

_____

_ _

_____

A Special Place

Think of a special place you have visited. Draw a picture of the special place. Then write a sentence about it.

_____

- -

_____

_____

- -

_____

A Favorite Day

The picture shows Ann's favorite day. Look at the picture.
Write a sentence about Ann's favorite day.

_____

- -

_____

- -

_____

- -

_____

Finish the Picture

Finish the picture. Draw what happens. Then write a sentence about the picture.

_____

- -

_____

_____

- -

_____

_____

- -

_____

Animal in a Tree

**Draw a picture of a bird or another animal in the tree.
Write a sentence about your picture.**

_____

- -

_____

- -

_____

Name _____ Date _____

Write About a Circus

Imagine that you are in a circus. What would you do? Draw a picture of yourself. Write a sentence to go with the picture.

_____

- -

_____

- -

_____

UNIT 2: Personal Story
Assessment

Read the story. Circle the words that tell the order in which things happen.

My family had fun at the summer fair yesterday. First, my brother rode a scary ride. Then, my sister and I got to pet a goat! The goat tried to bite my shirt. The goat made us laugh! Last of all, I won a prize at the fair. I can't wait for the next fair!

Write the sentence that tells what the topic is.

Topic Sentence

_____

- -

_____

_____

- -

_____

Name _____ Date _____

Studying a Personal Story

- A personal story tells about something you have done.
- It can tell how you feel about something.
- A story tells what happened in order.

Read the story. Draw a line under the words that show it is a personal story. Draw a line around the words that tell the order in which things happen.

My family and I love holidays. We think Thanksgiving is the best. All my grandparents come to our house. First, we sit at a very long table. Then, my sister brings in the food. The turkey always smells great! It tastes even better. After dinner we sing songs. We have a good time. Last of all, we hug each other good-bye. I can't wait for the next holiday!

Write a sentence about your favorite holiday.

_____

- -

_____

- -

_____

Grouping Ideas by Topic

- In a personal story, good writers tell about one topic.
- Good writers use only details that tell about the topic.

Read the story about animal movies. Write the sentence that tells what the topic is. Draw a line under the details that tell about the topic.

I like many movies about animals. In one movie I saw deer, bears, and foxes in a forest. Another movie was a cartoon about mice and pigs. The best animal movie I ever saw took place in the jungle. It was about a parrot that saved a tiger's life. It was really great!

Topic Sentence

_____

- -

_____

- -

_____

Write a sentence to add to the story.

_____

- -

_____

- -

Name _____ Date _____

Using Synonyms

| • Good writers choose words to write exactly what they mean to say. |

Read each sentence. Choose the more exact word to finish the sentence.

(go, dash)

1. We _____ into the store before it rains.

(boxes, things)

2. There are many _____ on the shelves.

(fruit, apples)

3. My dad buys some ripe _____ .

(soft, fuzzy)

4. I find some _____ peaches.

(cheerful, good)

5. I feel _____ when I'm with my dad.

(laugh, giggle)

6. My dad makes me _____ .

Name _____ Date _____

Proofreading a Personal Story

PROOFREADING HINT
- Be sure that the word I is a capital letter.
- Be sure that each sentence begins with a capital letter.
- Be sure that each sentence ends with an end mark.

Read the story. Use the Proofreader's Marks to correct at least eight mistakes.

One day my family and I went to an apple orchard. we went to pick fresh apples. first, i got a big basket. next, I picked some ripe apples off the trees I put them in the basket After about an hour, i was too hungry to keep going. that's when i bit into a juicy, red apple The sweet, ripe apple tasted better than anything else in the world.

Proofreader's Marks
≡ Use a capital letter.
⊙ Add a period.
∧ Add something.
✄ Take out something.
⌒ Change something.
◯ Check the spelling.

Write About a Pet

Imagine you have a pet. Where does your pet sleep? What does your pet play with? Write a story about your pet.

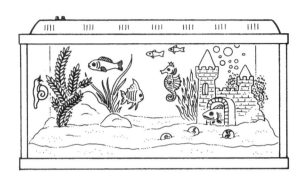

_____

- -

_____

- -

_____

- -

_____

- -

_____

- -

_____

Name _____ Date _____

Fun With Your Neighbors

Think of something you like to do
with your neighbors. Draw a picture
of you doing it. Then write a story
to go with your picture. Use the
words <u>men</u>, <u>women</u>, and <u>children</u> in
your sentences.

Name _____ Date _____

I'm Late!

Think of a time when you were late.
Write a story about what happened.

_____

- -
_____

- -
_____

- -
_____

- -
_____

- -
_____

- -
_____

Name _____ Date _____

Write About Your Feelings

Choose a feeling you sometimes have. Draw a picture of yourself with that feeling. Below the picture write a story about a time you felt that way.

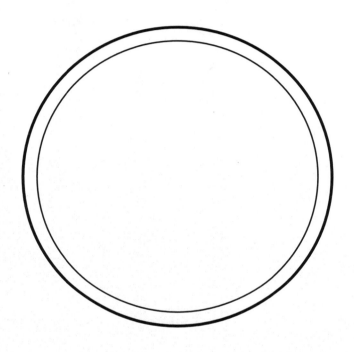

_____

- -

_____

_____

- -

_____

_____

- -

_____

_____

- -

Name _____ Date _____

Write About a Sport

Think about a game you and a friend like to play. Write a story about a time you played the game.

_____

- -

_____

- -

_____

- -

_____

- -

_____

In a Show

Imagine that you are going to be in a show. With a partner, make a list of things you might do in a show. Choose one thing from the list. Write a story about doing that thing in a show.

_____   _____
-        -
_____   _____

_____   _____
-        -
_____   _____

_____   _____
-        -
_____   _____

What I Might Do in a Show

_____
- -
_____

_____
- -
_____

Name _____ Date _____

Let's Eat!

Work with a partner. Think of one of
your favorite foods. Close your eyes
and picture it in your mind. Then write
words in the chart to describe the food.

Food: _____

```
❖ ❖ ❖ ❖ ❖ ❖ ❖ ❖ ❖ ❖ ❖ ❖ ❖ ❖ ❖ ❖ ❖ ❖ ❖ ❖ ❖ ❖ ❖ ❖ ❖ ❖ ❖ ❖ ❖ ❖ ❖ ❖ ❖
❖  _____      _____  ❖
❖  - - - - - - - - - - - - - - -      - - - - - - - - - - - - - - -  ❖
❖  _____      _____  ❖
❖  _____      _____  ❖
❖  - - - - - - - - - - - - - - -      - - - - - - - - - - - - - - -  ❖
❖  _____      _____  ❖
❖  _____      _____  ❖
❖  - - - - - - - - - - - - - - -      - - - - - - - - - - - - - - -  ❖
❖  _____      _____  ❖
❖ ❖ ❖ ❖ ❖ ❖ ❖ ❖ ❖ ❖ ❖ ❖ ❖ ❖ ❖ ❖ ❖ ❖ ❖ ❖ ❖ ❖ ❖ ❖ ❖ ❖ ❖ ❖ ❖ ❖ ❖ ❖ ❖
```

Write a story about your favorite food.

_____

- -

_____

_____

- -

_____

_____

- -

_____

My Favorite Holiday

Think of four things that happen on your favorite holiday. Draw four pictures to show these things. Then write a story that tells what happens. Use your pictures to help you.

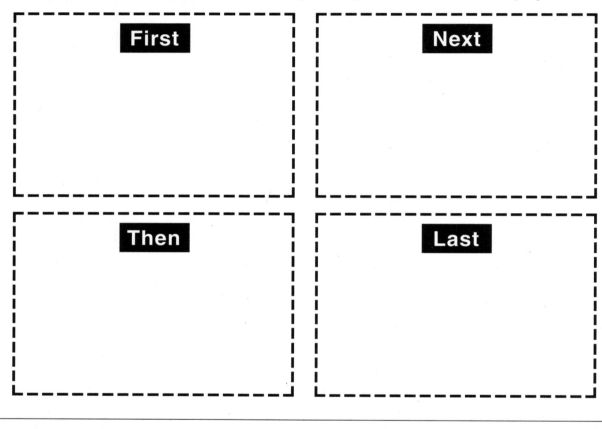

First

Next

Then

Last

UNIT 3: Friendly Letter
Assessment

Read the letter. Underline these parts of the letter. Use different colors.

1. heading-yellow   **2.** signature-blue   **3.** closing-red

Then answer the question about the letter.

October 22, 1999

Dear Aunt Rosa,

    The sweater you knitted for my birthday is great! The fall days here have been chilly. It's nice to have a new warm sweater to wear. It is just the right size. Thank you, Aunt Rosa.

Love,
Juan

4. Who wrote the letter?

_____

- -

_____

Studying a Friendly Letter

A friendly letter has five parts.

Read the letter. Draw a line around each part of the letter. Use different colors.

heading-red

closing-yellow

greeting-blue

signature-orange

body-green

July 27, 1998

Dear Chris,

    My family and I moved to a new house. I go to another school now. My new teacher is nice. I have a friend named Jimmy. He is in my class. Jimmy and I are on the same baseball team. Do you like to play baseball?

              Your friend,

              Richard

Name _____ Date _____

Picturing Events

- Good writers picture events in their minds before they write about them.

Finish the pictures. Draw what happens. Then write what happens.

1.

_____

_ _ _ _ _ _ _ _ _ _ _ _ _ _ _ _ _ _

_____

_ _ _ _ _ _ _ _ _ _ _ _ _ _ _ _ _ _

_____

2.

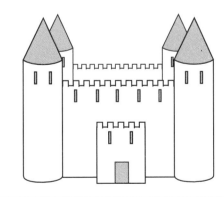

_____

_ _ _ _ _ _ _ _ _ _ _ _ _ _ _ _ _ _

_____

_____

_ _ _ _ _ _ _ _ _ _ _ _ _ _ _ _ _ _

Writing for Your Reader

- Good writers decide <u>who</u> will read their writing.
- Good writers decide <u>why</u> they are writing.

Read the letter. Then answer the questions about it.

October 22, 1998

Dear Grandma,
   The sweater you knitted for my birthday is great! The fall days here have been chilly. It's nice to have a new warm sweater to wear. It is just the right size. Thank you, Grandma.

Love,
Emily

1. To whom did Emily write the letter?

_____

- -

_____

2. Why did Emily write the letter?

_____

- -

_____

3. What did Emily write that Grandma might like to read?

_____

- -

_____

Name _____ Date _____

Joining Sentences

- Writers often join two sentences into one. The new sentence says the same thing in fewer words.

Read each pair of sentences. Use the word <u>and</u> to join the two sentences into one.

Andy talks. Andy tells jokes.

_____

1. _____

He dances. He sings.

_____

2. _____

Andy writes plays. Andy acts them out.

_____

3. _____

_____

He gets applause. He gets cheers.

_____

4. _____

_____

_____

Proofreading a Friendly Letter

PROOFREADING HINT
- Check for commas in the heading, greeting, and closing.
- Check for capital letters in the heading, greeting, and closing.
- Check your spelling.

Read the letter. Add <u>commas</u> (,) where they are needed. Correct at least six mistakes. Use the Proofreader's Marks.

February 13 1999

dear Tanya

    I had fun at your house last week! I'm so bezy at school now. I'm in the class play. I am a bear in the play My costume is brown and fuzzy. have you ever been in a play?

                your friend

                Brenda

Proofreader's Marks

≡	Use a capital letter.
⊙	Add a period.
∧	Add something.
✗	Take out something.
⌒	Change something.
◯	Check the spelling.

Name _____ Date _____

Write About Summer Fun

Write a letter to a friend. Tell your friend what you like to do in the summer.

41

Write a Group Letter

Read the letter below. On a separate sheet of paper, work with a group of classmates to write a letter back to Michael. Each person should write one sentence in the body of the letter. Read the letter to your class.

July 27,1999

Dear Friend,

My family and I moved to a new house. I go to a new school now. My new teacher is nice. I have a friend named Justin. He is in my class. Justin and I are on the same baseball team. Do you like to play baseball?

Your friend,

Michael

Name _____ Date _____

Letter Ideas

Think of two people to whom you might write a letter. At the top of each part, write a person's name. Under each name write why you are writing. Then write three ideas that the person would like to read.

Write About a Visit

Think about a time you visited a friend or a relative. Write a letter to that friend or relative telling what you enjoyed about the visit.

A Season Letter

With a partner, choose your favorite season. It might be fall, winter, spring, or summer. Draw a picture of your favorite season. Then write a letter to your teacher telling something you would like to do during your favorite season.

My Favorite Season

A Letter to a Famous Person

Write a letter to a famous person. Tell that person something about yourself. Ask the person questions about what he or she does. Read your letter to the class.

Name _____ Date _____

Invite a Friend

Write a letter to invite someone to do something or to go somewhere. Use these ideas or use your own ideas.

a class play   to come to your house

Thank You Very Much

With a partner, make a list of people at school who have helped you. Then pick someone from the list and write him or her a thank-you note.

Name _____ Date _____

UNIT 4: Paragraph That Describes
Assessment

Read the paragraph. Then answer the questions.

I just love a parade. I like to see the band march by. The uniforms shine with brass buttons and gold braid. The loud music always makes me want to clap my hands. I also like to see the floats. The floats with storybook characters are the best.

1. What is the topic of the paragraph?

_____

_____

2. Which words describe the band?

_____

_____

_____

3. Write a sentence to add to the paragraph.

_____

_____

_____

Studying a Paragraph That Describes

 • A paragraph that describes tells what someone or something is like.
- The topic sentence names the topic.
- The other sentences give details about the topic.

Read the paragraph. Then answer the questions.

Many birds visit my backyard. Red cardinals make nests in our bushes. Many tiny hummingbirds buzz around the flowers in our garden. Robins chirp sweetly to wake me in the morning.

1. What is the topic of the paragraph?

_____

- -

_____

2. Which words tell what the birds are like?

_____

- -

_____

3. Write a sentence to add to the paragraph.

_____

- -

_____

_____

- -

_____

Name _____ Date _____

Paying Attention to Details

- Good writers use their five senses to study what they will describe.
- They use words to describe what they notice.

Read each topic. Close your eyes and picture it in your mind. Then write words in the chart to describe the topic.

1. **Topic:**
an orange

Looks
_____

Feels
_____

Tastes
_____

Smells
_____

Sounds
_____

2. **Topic:**
a hamburger

Looks
_____

Feels
_____

Tastes
_____

Smells
_____

Sounds
_____

Unit 4: Paragraph That Describes
Writing Styles 2, SV 8055-3

Using Colorful Words

- Good writers choose colorful words to tell what something is like.

Read the beginning of the paragraph. The topic is kitchens. Write two more detail sentences. Use colorful words. Choose words from the box or use your own words.

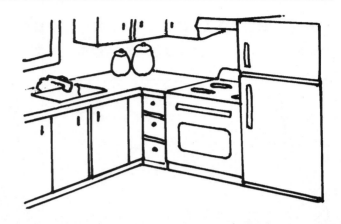

cozy

juicy

fresh

delicious

warm

yummy

sweet

shiny

The kitchen is the best room in a house. It smells like homemade bread and spices.

_____

- -

_____

- -

_____

- -

_____

- -

Adding Describing Words to Sentences

Writers can make a sentence clearer. They tell what someone or something is like. Find the nouns. Think of words that describe the nouns to add to each sentence. Write the new sentences.

The clown wears a hat.

1. _____

A lion jumps through a hoop.

2. _____

A monkey rides on an elephant.

3. _____

Proofreading a Paragraph That Describes

PROOFREADING HINT
- Be sure to indent your paragraph.
- Be sure each sentence begins with a capital letter.
- Check your spelling.

Read the paragraph. Correct at least six mistakes. Use the Proofreader's Marks.

Don't you just love a parade? I like to see the band march by. the uniforms shine with brass buttons and gold braid. The loud musik always makes me want to clap and stamp my feet. i also like to see the floats. The floats with storybook characters are the best. the kings and queens in purple velvet are so beautiful Sometimes there are people dressed up like giant animals. the big furry bears and long slithery snakes always make me laff.

Proofreader's Marks
≡ Use a capital letter.
⊙ Add a period.
∧ Add something.
✗ Take out something.
∧ Change something.
○ Check the spelling.

Write About a Zoo

Draw a picture of a zoo. Make a list of the details in your picture. Then write a sentence that tells the main idea.

_____   _____
- - - - - - - - - - - - - - - - -   - - - - - - - - - - - - - - - - -
_____   _____
_____   _____
- - - - - - - - - - - - - - - - -   - - - - - - - - - - - - - - - - -
_____   _____

Main Idea _____

- -
_____
_____
- -
_____

55

Name _____ Date _____

Write About a Place You Like

Think of a place you like. Draw a picture of the place. Then write three sentences to describe it.

Name _____ Date _____

Describe a Movie

Talk with a friend about a movie you both like. Write the name of the movie. Choose your favorite scene. Write a paragraph that describes your favorite scene.

_____

- -

_____

_____

- -

_____

- -

_____

- -

_____

- -

_____

- -

_____

Describe an Exciting Game

Think of an exciting game that you saw or that you have played. Write four sentences about the game.

_____

- -

_____

- -

_____

- -

_____

- -

_____

- -

_____

- -

A Day at a Lake

Work with a partner. Imagine that you are having fun at a lake. Think about how it looks, how it smells, and how it sounds. Write four sentences telling what you do.

_____

- -

_____

- -

_____

- -

_____

- -

_____

- -

_____

Describe a Circus

Imagine that you are at a circus. Write three sentences to tell what you see. Use words to describe the nouns. Then make a poster that shows the circus.

_____

- -

_____

- -

_____

- -

_____

- -

_____

Write a Room Riddle

Think about a room in your house or at school. Write sentences to describe it. Do not tell the name of the room. Read your sentences to a friend. Can your friend guess the name of the room?

_____

_____

_____

_____

_____

_____

_____

_____

Write About Bugs

Write four sentences about bugs. Use describing words that tell about the shape and color of the bugs.

Name _____ Date _____

Write About a Snack

Think about a snack you shared with friends. Close your eyes and picture it in your mind. Then write words in the chart to describe the snack.

Looks _____   _____

- - - - - - - - - - - - - - - - -   - - - - - - - - - - - - - - - - -

_____   _____

Feels _____   _____

- - - - - - - - - - - - - - - - -   - - - - - - - - - - - - - - - - -

_____   _____

Tastes _____   _____

- - - - - - - - - - - - - - - - -   - - - - - - - - - - - - - - - - -

_____   _____

Smells _____   _____

- - - - - - - - - - - - - - - - -   - - - - - - - - - - - - - - - - -

_____   _____

Write sentences to describe the snack.

_____

- -

_____

- -

_____

- -

_____

Unit 4: Paragraph That Describes
Writing Styles 2, SV 8055-3

Name _____ Date _____

Who Am I?

Draw a picture of yourself sitting at your desk. Then write sentences to go with your picture.

Tell what you can taste, smell, feel, and hear. Use describing words in your sentences.

_____

- -

===

- -

_____

- -

Unit 4: Paragraph That Describes
© Steck-Vaughn Company

64

Name _____ Date _____

Write a Travel Report

Write about your city or town. Tell visitors about the special places they can see.

_____

- -

_____

- -

_____

- -

_____

- -

_____

Picture a Place

Think about the places in these pictures. Pick one of the places. Write a paragraph that describes what that place is like.

on a busy city street

on a beach

_____

- -

_____

- -

_____

- -

_____

- -

_____

- -

_____

- -

_____

UNIT 5: Story
Assessment

Read the story. Then answer the questions.

A Long Night

Lateisha got into bed. She lay down, but she was too tired to sleep. She tried counting sheep. She tried reading a book. Nothing worked.

At six o'clock in the morning, Lateisha gave up and got out of bed. She showered and dressed. When she started to eat her cereal, Mother asked why Lateisha was up so early. Mother told her it was Saturday. Without saying a word, Lateisha went back to bed.

1. What is the title?

_____

- -

_____

2. What is the problem?

_____

- -

_____

- -

_____

3. Who are the characters?

_____

- -

_____

Studying a Story

- A story has a beginning, a middle, and an ending.
- A story is often about solving a problem.
- A story has a title.

Read the story. Then answer the questions.

The Hole

One day a small boy was walking down the street. Suddenly he fell down a hole. It was a very deep, dark hole. The small boy couldn't see. He was really scared. What did he do? He fell asleep, of course!

A few hours later, the boy was awakened by singing. The voices were high-pitched and squeaky. Then the boy saw hundreds of tiny candles.

They were being carried by hundreds of tiny mice. They led him to an underground elevator. The boy went up. He was back on the street!

1. What is the title?

_____

- -

2. Who are the characters?

_____

- -

3. What is the problem?

_____

- -

4. How is the problem solved?

_____

- -

Thinking About What Might Happen

- Good writers create an interesting problem in the beginning of a story.
- Then they plan what will happen to solve the problem.

Read the beginning of the story. Then fill in the chart.

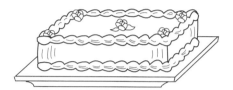

A Birthday Surprise

Aunt Sally would be ninety years old tomorrow. She had lived a long time, and she was very wise. My older sister and I wanted to do something special for Aunt Sally's birthday. We planned to bake her the most beautiful birthday cake she had ever seen. Every time we went into the kitchen, though, Aunt Sally was there!

Problem
_____
_____
_____
_____

How to Solve
_____
_____
_____
_____

Using Enough Details

- Good writers use enough details to help readers picture what happens in a story.

Read the paragraph. Then write it again. Add details to tell what John sees.

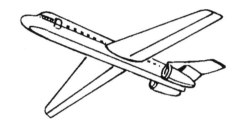

John could feel the plane taking off. He looked out the window.

_____

- -

_____

- -

_____

- -

_____

- -

_____

- -

_____

- -

_____

Proofreading a Story

PROOFREADING HINT
- Be sure each sentence begins with a capital letter.
- Be sure each sentence ends with an end mark.
- Check your spelling.

Read the story. Correct at least six mistakes. Use the Proofreader's Marks.

Proofreader's Marks
≡ Use a capital letter.
⊙ Add a period.
∧ Add something.
✗ Take out something.
⌃ Change something.
○ Check the spelling.

What a Day!

Arnold climbed the stairs. He was very tired. he could not keep his eyes open. School had been tuff that day. The soccer game had been tuffer.

Arnold got into bed. He lay down, but he was too tired to sleep. he tried counting sheep. he tried reading a book. Nothing worked.

At six o'clock in the morning, Arnold gave up and got out of of bed. He got washed and dressed. when he started to eat breakfest, his mother asked why he was up so early. She told him it was Saturday. Without saying a word, Arnold went back to bed

A Story About Foxes

Read the sentences. Then tell what the foxes do next. Finish the story.

Two foxes walk to the park. They sit on a bench. They eat their lunch.

_____

- -

_____

_____

- -

_____

_____

- -

_____

_____

- -

_____

_____

- -

_____

_____

- -

Write About Being a Cat

Imagine that you are a cat. Think about how you look. What do you do? Write a story about being a cat.

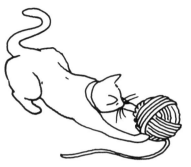

_____

_____

_____

_____

_____

_____

Write About Being a Rabbit

Read the story. Then write a story about what else could happen to Pinky, Spot, and Fluffy.

My favorite movie is on now. Real rabbits are in the movie. Their names are Pinky, Spot, and Fluffy. Once Spot got his tail stuck in a fence. Pinky and Fluffy helped him.

_____

_____

_____

_____

_____

_____

Write About Waiting

Think of a time you had to wait for someone else. Write a story about what happened.

_____

- -

_____

- -

_____

- -

_____

- -

_____

- -

_____

- -

_____

Finish the Story

**Read the story. What do you think
is in the bag? What do you think
happens next? Finish the story.
Tell what happens.**

    Last night I saw a huge monster.
I saw a bag in the monster's hand.
The monster gave me the bag.
I saw something funny inside.
I gave it to my sister.

Name _____ Date _____

Write a Story Beginning

Write good beginning sentences for a story about going into outer space. Draw a picture to go with your sentences.

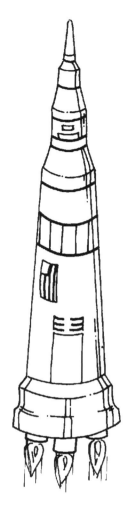

_____

- -

_____

- -

_____

- -

_____

- -

_____

- -

_____

- -

_____

- -

Write Animal Facts

Draw a picture of an animal. Then use the sentences below to write about it. Write exact words in place of the underlined words.

The <u>animal</u> can <u>move</u>.

The <u>animal</u> eats <u>food</u>.

_ _

_ _

_ _

_ _

Name _____ Date _____

Characters and Settings

Look at the pictures below. Look at the settings. Choose one character and one setting. Write a story about it.

Characters

Sammy Seal

Shawn

Kim

Settings

on a planet in the future
yesterday on a farm
at a beach in winter

_____

- -

_____

- -

_____

- -

_____

- -

_____

- -

_____

Solving a Problem

Many stories have an interesting problem that must be solved. Read the story. With a friend, write an ending to the story.

You make friends with a dinosaur and bring it to school. The dinosaur does not know how to act in school.

_____

- -

_____

_____

- -

_____

_____

- -

_____

_____

- -

_____

_____

- -

_____

Name _____ Date _____

Writing Styles 2, SV 8055-3

UNIT 6: How-to Paragraph
Assessment

Read the paragraph. Then answer the questions.

Sewing on a button can be easy. First, get a needle and thread. You will also need the button and a piece of clothing. Choose a thread color to match the clothing. Next, thread the needle. Then, sew on the button tightly. Last, make a knot in the thread. Cut the thread.

1. What is the topic sentence?

_____

_____

2. What is the first step?

_____

_____

_____

3. What things do you need to sew on a button?

_____

_____

_____

Studying a How-to Paragraph

- A how-to paragraph tells how to make or do something.
- The topic sentence names the topic of the paragraph.
- The detail sentences explain the steps in order.
- The paragraph is indented.

Read the paragraph. Draw a line under the topic sentence. Then draw a line around the words that tell the order of the steps.

    This is a simple way to wrap a gift. First, get wrapping paper, scissors, and tape. Next, cut the paper to fit all the way around the gift. Then, put the paper together around the middle of the gift. Tape the paper. Last, fold the paper up and over the ends of the gift. Tape it closed.

Write the things you need to wrap a gift.

Connecting Ideas in Sequence

- In a how-to paragraph, good writers tell the steps in the correct order.

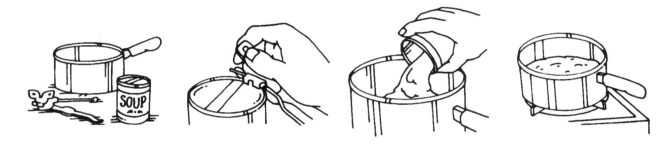

Look at the pictures. Then write the four steps.

How to Make Soup

1. _____

2. _____

3. _____

4. _____

83

Name _____ Date _____

Getting the Reader's Interest

- Good writers use good beginning sentences to interest their readers.

Read the story beginnings. Draw a line under the better one.

1. a. Albert waded through the swamp. The alligator was close behind him. Albert's heart pounded like a drum.

   b. Albert walked in the swamp. An alligator was following him. Albert felt scared.

2. a. The skyscraper was tall and shiny. It looked like a steel cube against the sky. I thought it was beautiful.

   b. The building was tall and gray. It stood out against the sky. It was interesting to look at.

3. a. One day we walked into a garden.

   b. One day we tiptoed into a strange garden. There were giant red and yellow flowers everywhere.

Unit 6: How-to Paragraph
© Steck-Vaughn Company

84

Writing Styles 2, SV 8055-3

Name _____ Date _____

Joining Sentences

- Writers often join two sentences into one. The new sentence says the same thing in fewer words.

Read each pair of sentences. Use the word <u>and</u> to join the two sentences into one. You may need to change the verb to go with your new sentence.

Bob likes to sled. Jasmine likes to sled.

1. _____

Tran goes with them. Carlos goes with them.

2. _____

Carlos packs a lunch. Bob packs a lunch.

3. _____

Bob sleds all day. Jasmine sleds all day.

4. _____

Bob is tired. Jasmine is tired.

5. _____

Proofreading a How-to Paragraph

PROOFREADING HINT
- Be sure you indent your paragraph.
- Be sure each sentence begins with a capital letter.
- Be sure each sentence ends with an end mark.

Read the how-to paragraph. Use the Proofreader's Marks to correct at least eight mistakes.

sewing on a button can be eazy. First, get a needle and thread. you will also need the button and peece of clothing Choose a thread color to match the clothing. next, thread the needle then, sew on the button tightly. Last, make a knot in the thread. Cut the thread

Proofreader's Marks	
≡	Use a capital letter.
⊙	Add a period.
∧	Add something.
✄	Take out something.
⤳	Change something.
◯	Check the spelling.

Write the topic sentence correctly.

_____

- - - - - - - - - - - - - - - - - -

_____

- - - - - - - - - - - - - - - - - -

_____

How to Play a Game

Work with some classmates. Imagine that you are at a playground. You are going to play a playground game. Write a paragraph telling how to play the game.

Write About a Job

Think of a job you have to do. Draw a picture of yourself doing that job. Write sentences telling how to do the job.

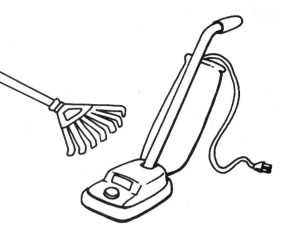

[drawing box]

_____

- -

_____

- -

_____

- -

_____

- -

_____

Name _____   Date _____

Plan a Garden

Work with a partner. Draw a picture of a garden you would both like. Write sentences that tell how you would make the garden.

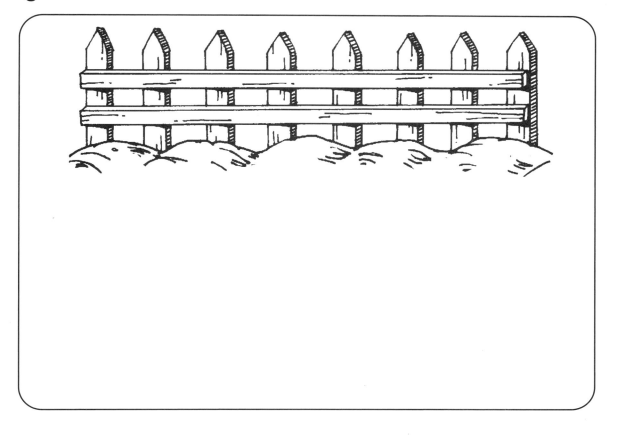

_____

- -

_____

- -

_____

- -

_____

- -

_____

Write About Work

Think of someone who has a job. Write sentences about what that person does at work. Tell how that person does one part of the job.

people at work

_____

- -

_____

- -

_____

- -

_____

_____

- -

_____

- -

_____

_____

- -

_____

- -

_____

Name _____ Date _____

Write About School

**Think of something you and your friends do at school.
Write directions for another student to follow.**

_____

- -

_____

_____

- -

_____

_____

- -

_____

_____

- -

_____

_____

- -

_____

_____

- -

_____

Name _____ Date _____

Write About Clown School

Imagine that you go to a school to learn to be a clown. Write sentences to tell a friend how to be a clown.

_____

- -

_____

- -

_____

- -

_____

- -

_____

- -

_____

- -

_____

- -

_____

Make a How-to Poster

Think about how you would do a chore, such as making a bed or washing the dishes. Picture the chore in four **steps**. Draw how to do a step in each part of this poster. Write a sentence for each step.

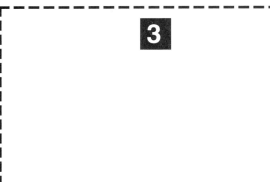

93

Name _____   Date _____

Write Steps

Think of something you know how to make. Write the steps in order. Then trade papers with a partner. Check to make sure the steps are in order.

How to Make _____

_____

1. _____

_____

_____

2. _____

_____

_____

3. _____

_____

WRITING STYLES: GRADE 2
ANSWER KEY

Unit 1: Sentence About a Picture

Assessment, P. 9
1. The girl eats pizza.
2. The robot walks a dog.
3. cereal

P. 10
1. The balloon goes up.
2. The room is a mess!
3. It's a windy fall day.
4. The girl is ready to eat.

P. 11
1. fruit bowl, 2 eggs, 1 glass
One person will eat breakfast.
2. ticket booth, roller coaster, Ferris wheel, children
The fair is open!

P. 12
1. Chimpanzees
2. hunting
3. Bananas
4. yellow
5. leap

P. 13

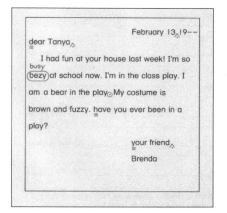

1. bears are big animals.
2. They may weigh 1000 pounds.
3. some live in cold places.
4. others like warm weather.

Unit 2: Personal Story

Assessment, P. 22
first, then, last of all
My family had fun at the summer fair yesterday.

P. 23
Underline: I, we, my, our
Circle: first, then, after, last of all

P. 24
Underline: In one movie I saw deer, bears, and foxes in a forest. Another movie was a cartoon about mice and pigs. The best animal movie I ever saw took place in the jungle. It was about a parrot that saves a tiger's life.
Topic sentence: I like many movies about animals.
Sentence added: Sentences will vary. Be sure that the detail supports the topic.

P. 25
1. dash
2. boxes
3. apples
4. fuzzy
5. cheerful
6. giggle

P. 26

One day my family and I went to an apple orchard. we went to pick fresh apples. first, i got a big basket. next, I picked some ripe apples off the trees. I put them in the basket. After about an hour, i was too hungry to keep going. that's when i bit into a juicy, red apple. The sweet, ripe apple tasted better than anything else in the world.

Unit 3: Friendly Letter

Assessment, P. 35
1. yellow: October 22, 1999
2. blue: Juan
3. red: Love,
4. Juan

P. 36
red: July 27, 1998
blue: Dear Chris,
green: body of letter
yellow: Your friend,
orange: Richard

P. 37
Responses will vary. Be sure that pictures are complete and that sentences tell about the pictures.

P. 38
1. her grandmother
2. to thank her
3. Possible response: The sweater is warm and it fits.

P. 39
1. Andy talks and tells jokes.
2. He dances and sings.
3. Andy writes plays and acts them out.
4. He gets applause and cheers.

P. 40

February 13, 19--

dear Tanya,

    I had fun at your house last week! I'm so busy (bezy) at school now. I'm in the class play. I am a bear in the play. My costume is brown and fuzzy. have you ever been in a play?

        your friend,

        Brenda

Unit 4: Paragraph That Describes

Assessment, P. 49
1. I just love a parade.
2. uniforms shine with brass buttons and gold braid, loud music always make me want to clap my hands
3. Sentences will vary. Be sure that the detail supports the topic.

P. 50
Possible responses:
1. Many birds visit my backyard.
2. red, tiny, buzz, sweetly
3. Sentences will vary. Be sure that the sentence supports the topic.

P. 51
Responses will vary. Be sure each response is a detail that supports the topic and is categorized correctly.

P. 52
Responses will vary. Be sure the detail sentences include vivid adjectives.

P. 53
Responses will vary. Be sure each sentence includes adjectives.

P. 54

> ¶Don't you just love a parade? I like to see the band march by. the uniforms shine with brass buttons and gold braid. The loud (musik) [music] always makes me want to clap and stamp my feet. i also like to see the floats. The floats with storybook characters are the best. the kings and queens in purple velvet are so beautiful⊙Sometimes there are people dressed up like giant animals. the big furry bears and long slithery snakes always make me (laff) [laugh]

Unit 5: Story

Assessment, P. 67
1. A Long Night
2. Lateisha couldn't sleep.
3. Lateisha, Mother

P. 68
1. The Hole
2. a boy, tiny mice
3. The boy falls down a hole.
4. The mice show the boy a way out.

P. 69
Problem: Aunt Sally was in the kitchen.
How to Solve: Responses will vary. Accept all responses that tell a way to solve the problem.

P. 70
Responses will vary. Be sure responses include enough details to tell clearly what John sees.

P. 71

> ### What a Day!
>
> Arnold climbed the stairs. He was very tired. he could not keep his eyes open. School had been (tuff) [tough] that day. The soccer game had been (tuffer) [tougher].
>
> Arnold got into bed. He lay down, but he was too tired to sleep. he tried counting sheep. he tried reading a book. Nothing worked.
>
> At six o'clock in the morning, Arnold gave up and got out of of bed. He got washed and dressed. when he started to eat (breakfes) [breakfast], his mother asked why he was up so early. She told him it was Saturday. Without saying a word, Arnold went back to bed⊙

Unit 6: How-to Paragraph

Assessment, P. 81
1. Sewing on a button can be easy.
2. First, get a needle and thread.
3. needle, thread, button, piece of clothing

P. 82
Underline: This is a simple way to wrap a gift.
Circle: First, Next, Then, Last
Things you need: wrapping paper, scissors, tape

P. 83
Possible responses:
1. First, get a can of soup, a can opener, and a pot.
2. Next, open the soup can.
3. Then, pour the soup into the pot.
4. Last, heat the soup.

P. 84
1. a
2. a
3. b

P. 85
1. Bob and Jasmine like to sled.
2. Tran and Carlos go with them.
3. Carlos and Bob pack a lunch.
4. Bob and Jasmine sled all day.
5. Bob and Jasmine are tired.

P. 86

> ¶sewing on a button can be (eazy) [easy]. First, get a needle and thread. you will also need the button and (peece) [piece] of clothing⊙ Choose a thread color to match the clothing. next, thread the needle⊙ then, sew on the button tightly. Last, make a knot in the thread. Cut the thread⊙